Vegetarian Christmas Cookbook

Sarah Reed

First Edition 2014

INTRODUCTION

Every year more than four hundred million people celebrate Christmas.

Christmas celebrations start on Christmas Eves December 24 and continue on December 25.

Christmas traditions include attending mass, exchanging gifts and having dinner with family and friends.

Christmas dishes include meats and other ingredients that vegetarians choose to refrain from eating.

In today's society we have many people who are vegetarians who love celebrating Christmas. Vegetarian often miss out at the Christmas dinner party.

It can be a bit tricky to come up with good vegetarian recipes for Christmas to suit everyone, but a good range of options can be the solution.

If you are a vegetarian, this book is for you and if you are not but want to try some delicious recipes that exclude meats, this book is also for you.

This book includes delicious recipes from starters to main dishes and desserts.

DISCLAIMER

All rights Reserved:

Disclaimer and Terms of Use:

Effort has been made to ensure that the information in this book is accurate and complete, however, the author and the publisher do not warrant the accuracy of the information, text and graphics contained within the book due to the rapidly changing nature of science, research, known and unknown facts and internet. The Author and the publisher do not hold any responsibility for errors, omissions or contrary interpretation of the subject matter herein. This book is presented solely for motivational and informational purposes only.

First Edition 2014

TABLE OF CONTENTS

TYPES OF VEGETARIANS, A SHORT GUIDE FOR BEGINNERS

Many people choose to become vegetarians for various reasons; for health issues, to lose weight or to save the environment. If you are a vegetarian or decide to become vegetarian you do not have to fit on any category listed below; just eat what you feel comfortable with eating and enjoy.

Here is a guide:

Vegans are vegetarians that choose to exclude meats, dairy products and egg, including all animal-derived ingredients and processed foods that include these ingredients. Many others choose to avoid processed foods that may not include animal products such as some wines and sugar.

Lacto-ovo vegetarian are vegetarians that choose not to eating meats or animal flesh of any variety, but they consume eggs and dairy products. Ovo-vegetarians eat eggs but no dairy products; Lacto vegetarians consume dairy products but do not eat eggs or meats.

Flexitarian are those who eat mostly vegetarians, but from time to time they also eat meat.

Pescatarians are vegetarians that refrain from eating meats with the exception of fish.

Raw vegans are vegetarians that eat vegan food that have not been heated above 115 deg. F (46 deg. C).

Macrobiotic are vegetarians that consume unprocessed vegan foods and also fish on seldom occasions. Refined sugars and oil are also excluded. Macrobiotic vegetarians usually eat Asian vegetables and sea vegetables.

STARTERS

Lemony Walnut Chickpea Salad with Goat's Cheese

Ingredients:

- 14 oz. (400g) tin chickpeas, drained
- ½ small red onions thinly sliced.
- 2 oz. (50g) soft goat's cheese, crumbled
- 0.7oz. (20g) rocket, chopped
- 2oz. (50g) walnut, chopped
- 2 tablespoons mayonnaise
- 2 tablespoons freshly squeezed lemon juice
- Pinch salt
- Pinch black pepper

Method:

- In a bowl add chickpeas, onion, goat's cheese, rocket, and walnut.
- Pour the mayonnaise and combine well.
- Add lemon juice, salt and pepper and mix again.
- Serve with salad, or on pitta bread.

Nutritional Facts

Serves: 2
Calories: 318Cal
Fat: 28g
Carbohydrate: 42.2g
Fiber: 14.6g
Sugar: 4.7g
Protein: 26.8g

Naan, Spinach and Halloumi Bites

Ingredients:

- 2 tablespoons of butter
- 2 cloves garlic, crushed
- 2 teaspoons garam masala
- 4 naan bread
- 2 x 3oz.(80g) bags baby spinach, chopped
- 2 x 9oz.(250g) packs halloumi cheese, cut into cubes
- Salt and pepper to taste

Method:

- In a pan, add butter and melt.
- Add garlic and masala.
- Add spinach and cook until soft, add salt and pepper.
- Grill halloumi cubes and nann bread.
- Remove from grill and spread spinach mixture over the naan bread.
- Place halloumi cubes over the spinach mixture and cut bread into cubes to fit the cheese.
- Secure the cubes with cocktail sticks.

Nutritional Facts

Serves: 40
Calories: 95 Cal
Fat: 5 g
Carbohydrate: 8 g
Fiber: 1 g
Sugar: 1 g
Protein: 4 g

Stuffed Tomatoes with Tuna

Ingredients:

- 8 tomatoes, tops cut off, cored and seeded
- 2 hard-boiled eggs, shelled and chopped
- 2 cans of tuna, drained
- 3 tablespoons homemade mayonnaise or to taste
- 4 cloves garlic, minced
- ½ cup chopped fresh parsley
- Salt to taste
- Pepper to taste
- Lettuce leaf to garnish

Method:

- In a bowl, add tuna, mayonnaise, garlic and eggs, salt and pepper and mix well.
- Stuff the tomatoes with the mixture.
- Garnish with parsley.
- Serve on a bed of lettuce (optional).

Nutritional Facts

Serves: 16
Calories: 81 Cal
Fat: 4.5 g
Carbohydrate: 2.8 g
Fiber: 0.8 g
Sugar: 1.7 g
Protein: 7.3 g

Truffle Parsnip and Parmesan Bruschetta

Ingredients:

- 1 ciabatta or Panini roll, sliced into 12x 13/64inch(12 x 0.5 cm)
- 1 clove garlic, halved
- 2oz.(50g) butter
- 3 large parsnips, cored and cubed (1 cm each)
- 1 tablespoon truffle oil
- 2 tablespoon olive oil
- Rocket leaves
- 2oz.(50g) parmesan shaving (or vegetarian option)
- Salt and pepper to taste

Method:

- In a pan, at medium heat, toast bread slices on both sides until brown.
- Rub garlic over each portion of bread.
- In another pan, melt butter.
- Add parsnip cubes, salt and pepper.
- Cook for 20 minutes until golden and softened.
- In a food processor, add parsnip and oils.
- Puree and add salt and pepper. Set aside.
- Cover the slices of bread with a scoop of puree.
- Add some rocket leaves and parmesan shavings.
- Drizzle with oil (optional).

Nutritional Facts

Serves: 12
Calories: 112 Cal
Fat: 8g
Carbohydrate: 9g
Fiber: 2g

Sugar: 2g
Protein: 3g

Wild Mushroom and Port Brioche

Ingredients:

- 6 brioche rolls
- 2 tablespoons olive oil
- 8oz.(225g) chestnut mushrooms, halved
- 2 large field mushrooms, sliced
- 4oz.(115g) shiitake mushroom, halved
- 3 stick celery, finely chopped
- 1 onion, cut into wedges
- 2 clove garlic, crushed
- 10 fl. oz.(300ml) red wine
- 40 fl. oz. (1.2 l.) Hot vegetable stock
- 2 sprigs fresh thyme
- 1 tablespoons redcurrant jelly
- 5 fl. oz.(150ml) port
- Parsley to garnish

Method:

- Pre-heat oven to 400 deg. F (200 deg. C).
- In a pan add 1 tablespoon of oil and heat.
- Add mushrooms and fry for 4-5 minutes, until browned.
- Remove from the pan and set aside.
- In the same pan, at low heat, add celery, garlic and onion and fry for 5-6 minutes.
- Add wine, thyme, stock and bring to the boil.
- Cook for 30 minutes.
- Add redcurrant jelly and port and bring to the boil.
- Cook for further 10 minutes until the liquid is reduced and thickened.
- Remove thyme and add mushrooms and cook for 5 minutes.
- In the meantime, remove the tops of the brioche rolls.
- Scoop the dough from the center of the rolls.
- Place in the oven and grill for 5-7 minutes.

- Remove rolls from the oven and fill with mushroom mixture.
- Garnish with parsley and serve.

Nutritional Facts

Serves: 6
Calories: 365 Cal
Fat: 12g
Carbohydrate: 43 g
Fiber: 3g
Sugar: 3 g
Protein: 9 g

Falafel

Ingredients:

- 1pound 5oz. (600g) chickpeas, rinsed and drained
- 1 small onion, finely chopped
- 2 cloves garlic, minced
- 1 teaspoon dried parsley
- 2 teaspoons ground cumin
- 1/8 teaspoon ground turmeric
- ½ teaspoon baking powder
- 1 cup dry breadcrumbs
- ¾ teaspoon salt
- ¼ teaspoon ground black pepper
- 2 tablespoons fresh coriander
- Vegetable oil

Method:

- In a bowl, add chickpeas and mash.
- Add onion, coriander, garlic, parsley, turmeric, cumin, baking powder, breadcrumbs, pepper and salt and mix well.
- Using your hands, shape mixture into 18-24 balls.
- In a deep fryer, at   deg. F. (190 deg. C), heat oil.
- Fry balls until brown.
- Dry falafel on paper towels.
- Serve with salad.

Nutritional Facts

Serves: 6
Calories: 142Cal
Fat: 7.2g
Carbohydrate: 76.2g
Fiber: 18.7g

Sugar: 12.6g
Protein: 22.0 g

Raw Vegan Stuffed Mushrooms with Herbed Pate

Ingredients:

- ½ cup walnuts
- 2 cups of water
- 16 large Cremini mushrooms, stem removed
- ¼ cup nama shoyu
- 1 ½ cups broccoli florets
- 1 cup fresh cilantro, chopped
- 1 tablespoon fresh rosemary
- 2 tablespoons fresh parsley, chopped
- 2 tablespoons olive oil
- 2 tablespoons nutritional yeast
- 3 tablespoons pine nuts
- ¼ cup red onion, chopped
- ½ cup celery, diced
- Pinch cayenne
- Salt and pepper to taste

Method:

- In a bowl, add walnuts and 2 cups of water and soak for 20 minutes.
- In another bowl, add half the nama shoyu.
- Add mushrooms caps and coat them.
- Remove from the bowl and place them in a casserole dish and set aside.
- In the meantime, pour the remaining nama shoyu in a food processor.
- Add broccoli florets, cilantro, herbs, oil, yeast, pine nuts, onion, cayenne, salt and pepper.
- Pulse until the mixture is soft and creamy.
- Remove from food processor and mix with diced celery.

- Place the mixture on top of the mushroom caps and serve.

Nutritional Facts

Serves: 4-8
Calories: 109Cal
Fat: 6.0g
Carbohydrate: 11.3g
Fiber: 3.3g
Sugar: 7.5g
Protein: 1.3g

Butternut, Pecan, Ricotta and Sage Pasties

Ingredients:

- 2 pounds 3 oz. (1 kg) butternut squash, seed removed, peeled and cubed (1/2 inch or 1.5 cm)
- 1 red onion, thinly cut
- 2 tablespoons extra virgin olive oil
- 12 sage leaves, shredded
- 1 pound 12oz (800g) ready-made puff pastry
- 4 oz. (120g) pecans
- 1 pound (500g) ricotta
- 4 tablespoons pumpkin seed oil
- 1 free-range egg
- 3 tablespoons flour
- Salt
- Fresh grounded black pepper

Method:

- Preheat oven at 390 deg. F (198 deg. C).
- In a baking tray, lined with baking paper, add butternut squash, sage, olive oil and onion.
- Season with salt and pepper.
- Place in the oven and cook until squash is soft. Remove and set aside.
- Dust a work surface with some flour, cut the pastry into two pieces and roll each piece to a 24x8inches (60x20cm) rectangle.
- Cut out 3 circles from each piece using a plate (8 inches or 20cm diameter)
- Place circles in a baking tray and refrigerate for 20 minutes.
- In a bowl, add the squash, ricotta, pumpkin seed oil, pecans and mix carefully.
- Remove pastry circles from the fridge.

- In the meantime, in a bowl, add egg and salt and beat.
- Brush pastry circles on one side with the egg.
- Place a spoonful of the squash mixture at the center of each circle.
- Fold each circle in half and with a fork press to seal the edges.
- Place each pasty back in the baking tray, lined with baking paper.
- Brash the pasties with egg again and with a fork place few holes.
- Cook for 25-35 minutes until golden
- Allow to cool before serving

Nutritional Facts

Serves: 6
Calories: 509Cal
Fat: 739g
Carbohydrate: 115.1g
Fiber: 7.6g
Sugar: 5.6g
Protein: 27.2 g

Grilled Goat's Cheese with Cranberry Dressing

Ingredients:

- 2 red apples, thinly sliced
- 1 tablespoon water
- 3 tablespoons lemon juice
- 3 x3 ½ oz.(100g) goat's cheese, halved (horizontally)
- 2 tablespoons cranberry jelly
- 2 tablespoons olive oil
- 1 tablespoon clear honey
- 1oz.(25g) pecans
- 2 chicory heads, divided into leaves
- Handful radish sprouts (or watercress)

Method:

- In a large bowl, add water, apple slices and lemon juice and mix.
- In the meantime, heat grill at high temperature.
- Line grill with foil paper and place cheese skin down and grill for 4 minutes.
- In the meantime, in a bowl, add 2 tablespoons of the juice from the apple bowl.
- Throw away the rest of the juice.
- Add cranberry juice, honey and oil and mix.
- Remove cheese from grill and top with nuts.
- Return to grill for few more minutes.
- On a serving plate, add apples, radish, chicory and cover with melted cheese and nuts.
- Pour cranberry dressing and serve.

Nutritional Facts

Serves: 6
Calories: 200Cal

Fat: 15g
Carbohydrate: 10g
Fiber: 1g
Sugar: 9g
Protein: 8g

Spicy Steamed Mussels

Ingredients:

- 3 tablespoons oil
- 2 large onions, finely chopped
- 4 cloves garlic, finely chopped
- 3 teaspoons fresh ginger, finely chopped
- 3 fresh chilies, deseeded and chopped
- ½ teaspoon ground turmeric
- 3 teaspoons ground coriander
- Pinch of chili powder
- ½ teaspoon salt
- 1 cup water
- 2 pounds 3 oz. (1 kg) fresh mussels, scrubbed and beards removed
- 1 tablespoon fresh coriander leaves, chopped
- Lemon juice to taste.

Method:

- In a large pan, at medium heat, add oil and heat.
- Add garlic, onion and ginger
- Cook until onion is browned.
- Add chili, ground coriander, turmeric, and chili powder.
- Stir for 3 minutes and then add salt and water and bring to the boil.
- Reduce heat and boil for 5 minutes, covered.
- Add mussels and cook for further 10-15 minutes until shells are opened.
- Remove from heat and serve.
- Sprinkle with coriander, salt and lemon juice.

Nutritional Facts

Serves: 6

Calories: 234Cal
Fat: 10.6g
Carbohydrate: 12.6g
Fiber: 1.4g
Sugar: 2.4g
Protein: 20.5 g

Crayfish Cocktail

Ingredients:

- 1 pound (450g) cooked crayfish tails, peeled
- 6 tablespoons mayonnaise
- 3 avocados, cut into pieces
- 1 small iceberg lettuce, shredded
- 1 teaspoon ground sumac or cayenne pepper
- Juice of one lemon
- Lemon wedges

Method:

- In a bowl, add mayonnaise, 2 teaspoons of lemon juice and sumac and mix.
- In 6 serving glasses, add a layer of lettuce, a layer of avocado and crayfish.
- Sprinkle with some lemon juice.
- Top with mayonnaise and serve with lemon wedges.

Nutritional Facts

Serves: 6
Calories: 338Cal
Fat: 25.6 g
Carbohydrate: 14.6g
Fiber: 7.2 g
Sugar: 2.2 g
Protein: 15.5g

MAIN

Vegan Christmas tofu "turkey"

Ingredients:

- 4 pounds 7oz.(2 kg) extra firm tofu, crumbled
- 1 red onion, finely sliced
- 4 celery stick, chopped
- 7 ¾ oz.(220g) mushrooms, chopped
- 2 cloves garlic, crushed
- 1 teaspoon fresh sage, chopped
- 1 tablespoon fresh thyme, chopped
- 1 tablespoon fresh rosemary, chopped
- Salt to taste
- Fresh ground black pepper to taste
- 5 cups dried breadcrumbs
- 8 tablespoons sesame oil
- 6 tablespoons soy sauce
- 2 tablespoons miso paste
- 5 tablespoons orange juice
- ½ teaspoon orange rind
- 1 teaspoon mustard
- 3 sprigs fresh rosemary to serve

Method:

- Pre-heat oven at 400deg. F (200 deg. C)
- In a colander, lined with muslin or clean tea towel, add tofu.
- Cover with another piece of muslin and add a heavy weight on top
- Put the colander over a bowl and refrigerate for 2-3 hours.
- In a pan, add 2 tablespoons of sesame oil.
- Add onion, mushroom and celery and fry.
- Add garlic, rosemary, thyme, sage, salt and pepper.
- Mix and cook for 5 minutes.
- Add breadcrumbs and mix again. Set aside.

- In a bowl, add the remaining oil, miso paste, soy sauce, orange rind, orange juice and mustard and combine.
- Remove tofu from the refrigerator, remove the weight and discard the liquid.
- Scoop some of the tofu until 1 inch (2.5 cm) of tofu is left on the side of the colander.
- Keep the remaining tofu in a bowl.
- Add the mixture in the center of the tofu and cover with the scooped tofu. Press firmly.
- Place the tofu in a lined baking tray, shaping the tofu until is oval in shape.
- Brush tofu with oil, add rosemary sprigs and cover with foil paper.
- Place in the oven and cook for 1 hour.
- Remove foil paper, brush some more sesame oil and cook for further 1 hour or until golden
- Allow to cool for 5 minutes and serve.

Nutritional Facts

Serves: 10
Calories: 479Cal
Fat: 22.5g
Carbohydrate: 47.2g
Fiber: 5.3 g
Sugar: 6.5g
Protein: 25.6g

Vegetarian Lentil "Meat" Loaf

Ingredients:

- 5oz.(150g) green lentils
- 2oz.(50g) wheat germ
- 6oz.(175g) dried breadcrumbs
- 3oz.(75g) brown rice
- 2 eggs
- 1 large onion, diced
- 1 teaspoon dried thyme
- 3 ½ oz.(100g) tomato paste
- 2 teaspoons hot sauce or Tobasco
- 2 tablespoons tomato sauce
- 2 teaspoons vegemite
- 2oz.(50g) grated cheddar cheese

Method:

- Pre-heat oven at 350 deg. F (175 deg. C).
- In a pot, add lentils and water and cook as per the packet instructions.
- In another pot, add water and rice and cook as per the packet instructions.
- In a bowl, add lentils and mash.
- Add wheat germ, brown rice, eggs, breadcrumbs, onion, thyme, tomato sauce, tomato paste, cheese and vegemite and mix.
- Place the mixture in a loaf tray.
- Place in the oven and cook for 1 hour
- Remove from oven.
- Allow to cool for 5 minutes and serve.

Nutritional Facts

Serves: 6

Calories: 364Cal
Fat: 2.8g
Carbohydrate: 56.1g
Fiber: 12.0g
Sugar: 6.5g
Protein: 19.0g

Chestnut and Shallot Tatins with Mushroom and Madeira Sauce

Ingredients:

- 1pound 2oz.(500g) banana shallot, peeled, cut in half lengthways
- 4 teaspoons sunflower oil
- 2 teaspoons balsamic vinegar
- 1 ½ tablespoons light soft brown sugar
- 11oz.(320g) pack ready rolled puff pastry
- 3 ½ oz.(100g) vacuum-packed cooked chestnuts, quartered
- 2 teaspoons fresh thyme (extra to garnish)
- 3 tablespoons dried mushrooms
- 5oz.(140g) chestnut mushrooms, sliced
- 1 tablespoon butter
- 1 tablespoon plain flour (extra for dusting)
- 3 tablespoons Madeira
- Salt to taste
- Pepper to taste

Method:

- Pre-heat oven at 350 deg. F (180 deg. C).
- In a baking tray, add shallot pieces.
- Pour some oil, add salt and pepper and cook for 20-25 minutes.
- Remove from oven and sprinkle vinegar and sugar.
- Place the tray back to the oven and cook for another 10 minutes until soft.
- Set aside for 10 minutes.
- On a work surface, dust some flour and place the pastry.
- Roll the pastry and cut out four 5 1/8 inch. (13cm.) diam. circles.

- In four mini cake non-stick tins, distribute shallots and place them tightly.
- Sprinkle chestnuts, thyme leaves, salt and pepper.
- Place the puff circles on each tin and seal the edges against the tin.
- Using a fork prickle the pastry to make some holes.
- Wrap with cling film and refrigerate for 8 hours.
- Thirty minutes before removing the tins from the refrigerator prepare the mushroom and Madeira sauce.
- In a measuring jug, add dried mushroom and 6.7 fl. oz. (200ml) boiled water. Leave to rest for 20 minutes.
- Using a strainer, drain the mushroom and place the liquid in a bowl.
- Chop the mushroom and set aside.
- In a pan, over high heat, add oil and fry chestnut mushroom for 2-3 minutes.
- Reduce heat, melt the butter, add the drained mushrooms and flour and stir.
- Carefully pour the mushroom liquid, the Madeira and mix well.
- Bring the sauce to the boil and cook for 2 minutes.
- Heat the oven to 400 deg. F(200deg.C).
- On a baking tray, put the tins and cook for 20-25 minutes or until golden.
- Set aside for 5 minutes.
- Scoop the mushroom from the sauce and place on top of each pastry and pour sauce.
- Allow to cool for 5 minutes and serve with vegetables such as carrots and cabbage.

Nutritional Facts

Serves: 4
Calories: 390Cal
Fat: 22g
Carbohydrate: 37g
Fiber: 3g

Sugar: 10g
Protein: 7g

Parsnip, Cranberry and Chestnut Loaf

Ingredients:

- 1pound 3 ½ oz.(550g) parsnips, peeled and halved lengthways
- 3 onions, chopped
- 15g pack sage, shredded (keep 6 leaves to garnish)
- 4 tablespoons butter
- 7 oz.(200g) pack cooked chestnuts
- 3 ½ oz.(100g) walnuts
- 3 ½ oz(100g) breadcrumbs
- ½ teaspoon mace
- 1 egg, beaten
- 1 teaspoon honey
- 1 teaspoon sugar
- 1pound 3 ½ oz.(500g) cranberries
- 6oz.(175g) caster sugar

Method:

- In a pan, add 1 tablespoon butter and melt.
- Add onions and cook for 10-15 minutes.
- Add sage and stir for 1 minute.
- Remove from the pan, and place in a bowl. Set aside.
- In a food processor, add chestnuts and walnuts and pulse.
- Put the chestnut and walnuts in the bowl together with the onion.
- Add the beaten eggs, breadcrumbs, mace, 1 teaspoon of salt and pepper and mix.
- In a pan, over high heat, add sugar and cranberries and cook for 8-10 minutes.
- Keep cooking until sticky. Set aside.
- In a pot, add salted water and bring to the boil.

- Add parsnips and boil for 3 minutes. Drain. Cut parsnip to fit the loaf tin base tightly.
- Pre-heat oven at 350 deg. F (180 deg. C).
- Coat the parsnip with honey and 1 tablespoon of butter.
- In a 2 pounds (900g) loaf tin, greased and lined with baking paper, and greased again, add the parsnip.
- Chop the remaining parsnip and mix with the nut mixture.
- Add 1/3 of the nut mixture on top of the parsnip and compact and 1/3 of the cranberry sauce.
- Add the remaining nut mixture and compact again.
- Cover with foil and place in the oven to cook for 1 hour.
- Remove for the oven and turn out the loaf on serving plate.
- In a pan, melt some butter and cook the 6 sage leaves for a minute.
- Pour over the loaf together with extra cranberry sauce.

Nutritional Facts

Serves: 6
Calories: 819 Cal
Fat: 36 g
Carbohydrate: 117 g
Fiber: 15 g
Sugar: 71 g
Protein: 14 g

Christmas Veggie Wellington

Ingredients:

- 2oz.(60g) basmati rice, cooked in accordance with the instructions
- 1 lemon zest
- 1 onion, finely chopped
- 1 pound 5 oz. (600g) brown cap mushroom, sliced
- 2oz. (50g) butter
- 1 tablespoons fresh parsley, chopped
- 1 tablespoon fresh tarragon, chopped
- 1 tablespoon dried cranberries
- 2 free-range eggs, hard-boiled, chopped
- 1 pinch turmeric
- Salt to taste
- Fresh ground black pepper
- 9oz. (250g) ready-rolled pastry
- 1 free-range egg, beaten
- 1 tablespoon sesame seeds
- Vegetarian gravy to serve

Method:

- Pre-heat oven at 400 deg. F (200 deg. C).
- In a bowl, add the cooked rice, the lemon zest and turmeric.
- Cover and refrigerate.
- In a pan, over medium heat, heat butter.
- Add mushrooms and onion and cook for 3-4 minutes or until soft. Set aside.
- Remove the rice from the refrigerator and add cranberries, herbs, hard-boiled egg, salt and pepper and mix well.
- On a work surface, place the pastry and cut a rectangle 15inx8in (40cmx20cm).

- Place the rice mixture in the center and seal, bringing the sides together.
- Brush with beaten egg and place in the refrigerator for 30 minutes.
- Remove and sprinkle with sesame seeds.
- Place in the oven for 30 minutes or until golden.
- Allow to cool for 5 minutes, slice and serve with vegetarian gravy.

Nutritional Facts

Serves: 6
Calories: 304Cal
Fat: 15.7g
Carbohydrate: 31.8g
Fiber: 2.8g
Sugar: 3.2g
Protein: 10.2 g

Chestnut, Spinach and Blue Cheese Pastry

Ingredients:

- 2oz.(50g) butter
- 1 pound 2oz.(500g) leeks, thinly sliced
- 3 cloves garlic, thinly sliced
- 8oz (240g) baby spinach
- 14oz. (415g) can chestnut puree
- 4 eggs
- ½ nutmeg, finely grated
- 7oz.(200g) pack vacuum-packed whole cooked chestnuts, halved
- 3oz.(85g) fresh white breadcrumbs
- 8oz.(220g) blue Shropshire cheese, rind trimmed and diced
- 1 pound 2oz.(500g) puff pastry
- 17fl.oz.(500ml) vegetable stock
- 1 tablespoon corn flour
- 2 leeks, thinly sliced
- 10fl.oz.(300ml) cream

Method:

- In a pan, add butter and melt.
- Add garlic and leek and cook for 10 minutes until soft, covered.
- Remove from pan and place in a bowl.
- In the same pan, add spinach and cook until wilted.
- In the bowl with the leeks, add chestnut puree, nutmeg, spinach, 3 eggs, breadcrumbs, cheese and mix well.
- Place in the refrigerator for 1 hour.
- Pre-heat oven to 430deg.F (220 deg. C).
- On a work surface, sprinkle some flour and place pastry.
- Roll the pastry to a rectangle to the size of a large baking tray.
- Line the tray with baking paper and place the pastry.

- Brush the edges of the pastry with egg.
- Add the mixture in the center of the pastry and close the pastry by lifting the edges and pressing together.
- Brush with more egg and with a fork made few holes.
- Cook for 40-50 minutes until golden.
- Remove from oven.
- In the meantime, in a pan, add leeks and stock and boil for 5 minutes.
- Remove 2 tablespoons of the leek and discard.
- Add corn flour and blend with a hand mixer.
- Add cream.
- Slice the pastry and pour the sauce to serve.

Nutritional Facts

Serves: 8
Calories: 889Cal
Fat: 62g
Carbohydrate: 60g
Fiber: 8g
Sugar: 9g
Protein: 19 g

Sweet Potato and Leek Roulade with Christmas Stuffing

Ingredients:

Roulade

- 1 tablespoon olive oil
- 1 leek, finely chopped
- 2oz.(60g) butter
- 1/3 plain flour
- 10fl.oz.(300ml) milk
- 4 eggs whites
- 4 eggs yolk
- ½ cup grated cheddar cheese
- ¼ cup parmesan

Stuffing

- 1oz.(30g) unsalted butter
- 1 brown onion, finely chopped
- 2 cloves garlic, crushed
- 1 ½ cups fresh white breadcrumbs
- 1 tablespoons fresh sage, chopped
- 1 tablespoon parsley, chopped

Filling

- 1pound 2oz.(500g) sweet potato, peeled and chopped
- 1 tablespoon parsley, chopped
- ½ oz.(15g) unsalted butter
- 3 ½ fl. oz.(100ml) thin cream
- ½ teaspoon freshly grated nutmeg

Method:

Roulade

- Pre-heat oven at 350 deg. F (180 deg. C).
- In a pan, over medium heat, add oil.
- Add leeks and cook until soft. Remove from the pan.
- Clean the pan and add butter.
- Melt butter and add flour and cook for 1-2 minutes. Stir.
- Add milk, slowly and stir until thickened.
- Remove the pan from the heat.
- Add egg yolks and beat.
- In another bowl, add egg whites and whisk until stiff.
- Pour ¼ of the egg white to the flour mixture and fold slowly.
- Add leeks and cheddar cheese and combine.
- In a greased and lined Swiss roll pan (approx. 39x26cm), place the mixture.
- Place in the oven for 20-25 minutes or until golden and puffed.

Stuffing

- In the meantime, in a pan, over medium heat, add butter and melt.
- Add onion and cook until soft.
- Add garlic and breadcrumbs and cook for another 3-4 minutes.
- Add herbs, salt and pepper and stir.
- Allow to cool for 5 minutes and serve. Put to one side.

Filling

- In a pan or steamer, add sweet potatoes and cook until soft. Drain.
- Add butter, cream, nutmeg, salt and pepper and mash.

Preparation

- Place a clean tea towel over a work bench and sprinkle cheddar cheese.
- Turn the roulade over the tea towel (remove the baking paper).
- Spread the sweet potato mash over the roulade.
- Scatter the stuffing over the mash.
- Roll up the roulade using the tea towel from the longest side and ending with the seams-side down.
- Slice and serve.

Nutritional Facts

Serves: 6
Calories: 503Cal
Fat: 34g
Carbohydrate: 32g
Fiber: 3g
Sugar: 10 g
Protein: 16 g

Filo Strudel with Port Wine Sauce

Ingredients:

- 1 tablespoon olive oil
- 2 tablespoons of butter
- 5 ¼ oz. (150g) chestnut mushrooms
- 1 clove garlic
- Salt to taste
- Grounded black pepper
- 5 ¼ oz. (150g) leeks, trimmed and chopped
- 9oz.(250g) full-fat cream cheese
- 5 tomatoes, deseeded, skinned and chopped
- 18 pieces filo pastry (9inx6in or 23cmx15cm)

Sauce

- 2 tablespoons olive oil
- I onion, sliced
- 3oz. (75g) chestnut mushrooms, sliced
- 2 cloves garlic, minced
- 3 ½ fl. oz. (100 ml) vegetable stock
- 7 ¼ fl. oz. (200 ml) red wine
- Port
- 1 oz.(25g) butter, cubed

Method:

- In a pan, heat oil and melt butter.
- Add mushrooms and garlic and cook for 2 minutes.
- Drain well and keep aside.
- In the same pan, add leeks and cook for 2 minutes.
- Drain well and set aside.
- In a bowl, add cheese with salt and pepper and mix well.
- Add mushrooms, leeks and tomatoes and mix.
- Place in the refrigerator for 2 hours.

- Pre-heat oven at 400 deg. F (200 deg. C).
- On a work surface, dust some flour and lay the pieces of pastry.
- Brush with 3 layers of melted butter. The last layer only the edges.
- Remove the filling from the refrigerator and divide among the pieces of pastry.
- Fold the pastry into a tight parcel (length way, tacking the edges).
- In a baking tray, place the parcels and cook for 25 minutes.
- In the meantime, make the sauce.
- In a pan, heat oil.
- Add onion, garlic, mushrooms, salt and pepper and cook until soft.
- Pour stock and boil until almost all reduced.
- Add wine and pour and cook until reduced by half.
- Add butter to the sauce before serving.
- Put some sauce on serving plates.
- Remove strudels from the oven and place them over the sauce.

Nutritional Facts

Serves: 9
Calories: 612 Cal
Fat: 20.9 g
Carbohydrate: 86.1g
Fiber: 7.9 g
Sugar: 12.1g
Protein: 17.9 g

Beetroot and Gin Cured Salmon

Ingredients:

- 1pound 2oz.(500g) salmon fillet, skin on
- 2 tablespoons juniper berries
- ½ teaspoon black peppercorns
- 2 tablespoons sea salt
- 2 tablespoons sugar
- 5 tablespoons gin
- 5oz.(150g) raw beetroot, peeled and grated
- 3 tablespoons grated horseradish

Pickled cucumber

- 2 ½ oz.(75g) caster sugar
- 1 ½ teaspoons sea salt
- 6fl.oz.(175ml) white wine vinegar
- 10 peppercorns
- Rinds of ½ lemon
- 1 cucumber, deseeded, peeled and sliced
- 2 tablespoons sugar

Method:

- Place the salmon on a board or work surface and remove pin bones using a tweezers.
- In a baking tray, lined with baking paper, place the salmon skin down.
- Using a grinder or mortar and pestle, crush juniper and peppercorns.
- Place them in a bowl and combined with sugar, gin, beetroot and horseradish.
- Spread the mixture over the salmon and press firmly.

- With a cling film, wrap the salmon few times and refrigerate for 36 hours to 3 days (preferable).
- In the meantime, 1 hour before serving, prepare the pickled cucumber.
- In a pot, over medium heat, dissolve sugar and salt.
- Add white wine vinegar, peppercorns and lemon rind.
- Allow to cool down.
- Tip over the cucumber and cover.
- Refrigerate for 1 hour before serving.
- Remove the salmon from the refrigerator and un-wrap.
- Remove the marinade by using a blade or knife.
- With a sharp blade, slice the salmon and serve.

Nutritional Facts

Serves: 6
Calories: 247Cal
Fat: 5.3 g
Carbohydrate: 26.2g
Fiber: 1.1g
Sugar: g
Protein: 17.1g

Langosta Gratinada

Ingredients:

- 3 live rock lobsters (2 pounds or 1 kg each)
- 6 ½ oz. (185g) butter, softened
- 3 clove garlic, minced
- 1 tablespoons sweet paprika
- Pinch of chili flakes
- Handful of fresh coriander, chopped
- Sea salt to taste

Method:

- Place the lobsters in plastic bags and freeze for 1 hour.
- Remove from the freezer and with a sharp knife remove the membrane that joins the head to tail.
- Slice the lobster in half and remove the digestive system.
- Pre-heat oven to 250 deg. F (120 deg. C).
- In a bowl, add butter, paprika, garlic, coriander and chili flakes and mix.
- Add salt and pepper.
- In a baking tray, place lobsters flesh down.
- Place in the oven and cook for 7 minutes.
- In the oven grill, place the lobster, flesh up with some butter mixture.
- Grill for 4-5 minutes or until golden.
- Remove from oven and serve.

Nutritional Facts

Serves: 6
Calories: 249Cal
Fat: 25.2g
Carbohydrate: 1.2g
Fiber: 0g

Sugar: 0g
Protein: 0.5g

Octopus and Squid Casserole

Ingredients:

- 2pounds 3oz.(1kg) baby octopus
- 1pound 2oz. (500g) squid hoods
- 1 tablespoon olive oil
- 2 cloves garlic, crushed
- ½ teaspoon sambal oelek
- 20 baby onions
- 1 teaspoon fresh thyme, finely chopped
- 1 teaspoon fresh oregano, finely chopped
- 2 teaspoons fresh ginger, grated
- 1 teaspoon lime rind, grated
- 2 cans tomatoes (425g or 16oz. each)
- 1 teaspoon sugar

Method:

- Pre-heat oven at 350 deg. F (180 deg. C).
- Remove heads and beaks from octopus and cut in half.
- Cut squid hoods into ½ inch rings.
- In a large pan, at medium heat, heat oil.
- Add garlic, sambal oelek, herbs, onions, rind and ginger and cook for 2 minutes.
- Add octopus and squid and cook for another 5 minutes.
- Transfer to a casserole dish and add tomatoes with the juice and sugar and cover.
- Place in the oven for 30 minutes.
- Remove lid and simmer for another 45 minutes or until seafood is tender and sauce is thickened.
- Remove from oven and add olives and stir.
- Allow to cool for 5 minutes and serve.

Nutritional Facts

Serves: 6

Calories: 453 Cal

Fat: 7.3 g

Carbohydrate: 33.1 g

Fiber: 6.3 g

Sugar: 12.7 g

Protein: 61.3 g

SIDES

Easy Raw Pad Thai Salad

Ingredients:

- 2 zucchinis, sliced into strips (use a vegetables peeler)
- 2 cups bean sprouts
- ¾ cup nuts (almonds , peanuts or cashews), chopped
- 1 red bell pepper, sliced into strips
- 4 green onions, diced
- ½ cup fresh cilantro, chopped
- Juice from 1 lime
- 1 tablespoon raw, cold pressed olive oil
- ¼ teaspoon sea salt

Method:

- In a bowl, add all the vegetables and nuts.
- Pour oil and salt and mix well.

Nutritional Facts

Serves: 6
Calories: 161Cal
Fat: 11.7 g
Carbohydrate: 11.0g
Fiber: 3.0g
Sugar: 3.0 g
Protein: 6.7 g

Raw Salad with Vinaigrette (Vegan)

Ingredients:

- 2 ribs celery, diced
- 3 green onions, chopped
- ¾ cup snow peas, chopped
- 1 red bell pepper, sliced into strips
- 3 tablespoons fresh parsley, chopped
- 1 tablespoon balsamic vinegar
- 1 tablespoon apple cider vinegar
- 1 tablespoon agave nectar
- 1 tablespoon cold pressed sesame oil
- ¼ teaspoon sea salt

Method:

- In a bowl, add all the vegetables.
- In another bowl add nectar, sesame oil, the vinegars and whisk.
- Pour the liquid mixture over the vegetables, add salt and mix well.

Nutritional Facts

Serves: 6
Calories: 52Cal
Fat: 2.5g
Carbohydrate: 6.7 g
Fiber: 1.7g
Sugar: 4.7g
Protein: 1.1g

Stilton and Fig Salad with Honey-Thyme

Ingredients:

- 4 tablespoons clear honey
- 1 teaspoon thyme leaves
- 1 tablespoon cider vinegar
- 2 tablespoons repeseed oil (or vegetable oil)
- 2 tablespoons hazelnuts, toasted and chopped
- 1 small fennel bulb, trimmed and finely sliced
- 2 handful rocket leaves
- 7oz.(200g) Stilton cheese, thinly sliced
- 2 figs (ripe), halved
- Salt to taste

Method:

- In a pan, add honey and thyme and warm for 2 minutes. Set aside.
- In a bowl, add vinegar, oil, salt and whisk.
- Add fennel, rocket and hazelnuts and mix well.
- Between 4 plates, divide the cheese slices.
- Add a piece of fig and some salad on top on each plate.
- To serve drizzle some honey-thyme mixture.

Nutritional Facts

Serves: 4
Calories: 350 Cal
Fat: 26g
Carbohydrate: 15g
Fiber: 2g
Sugar: 15g
Protein: 14g

Spinach with Raisins, Pine Nuts and Breadcrumbs

Ingredients:

- 1 tablespoon olive oil
- 1 thick slice of bread whizzed to crumbs
- 1oz.(25g) pine nuts, toasted
- 2oz.(50g) raisins
- 1 clove, garlic, minced
- 9oz.(250g) spinach
- Salt and pepper to taste

Method:

- In a pan, at low heat, heat oil.
- Add garlic, breadcrumbs, salt and pepper.
- Cook until golden and crunchy.
- Remove from the pan and set aside.
- Add raisins and pine nuts and cook for 2 minutes.
- Add spinach and cook until wilted.
- On a serving dish, add the breadcrumbs mixture, the nuts/raising mixture and spinach.

Nutritional Facts

Serves: 4
Calories: 197 Cal
Fat: 10g
Carbohydrate: 22g
Fiber: 3g
Sugar: 14g
Protein: 6g

Super Food Nirvana Salad

Ingredients:

- 5 cups baby spinach
- 1 cup cooked quinoa
- 1 cup fresh strawberries, halved
- ½ cup blueberries
- ½ cup raspberries
- 2 kiwi fruits, peeled and sliced
- 2 cups beets, diced
- ½ cup sunflower seeds
- ¼ cup golden flax seeds

For dressing:

- 1 tablespoon olive oil
- ½ cup balsamic vinegar
- ¼ cup Acai berry juice
- ¼ cup blueberries
- ¼ cup strawberries
- ¼ teaspoon sea salt
- ¼ teaspoon pepper

Method:

- In a large bowl, add baby spinach, quinoa, strawberries, blueberries, raspberries, kiwi fruits, beets, sunflower seeds, golden flax seeds and toss well.
- Make the dressing by placing the olive oil, vinegar, acai berry juice, blueberries, strawberries in a food processor and blend until smooth.

- Pour the mixture over the salad and toss again.
- Place in the refrigerator.
- Allow for 20-25 minutes to cool.
- Serve chilled.

Nutritional Facts

Serves: 4
Calories: 200Cal
Fat: 4.2g
Carbohydrate: 35.2g
Fiber: 8.2g
Sugar: 11.3g
Protein: 7g

DESSERTS

Classic Christmas Pudding

Ingredients:

- 2oz.(50g) blanched almonds, chopped
- 2 Bramley cooking apples, cored, peeled and sliced
- 7oz. (200g) box candied peel, chopped
- 1 whole nutmeg, grated (3/4 of it)
- 2 pounds (1 kg) raisins
- 5oz.(140g) plain flour
- 3 ½ oz.(100g) soft breadcrumbs
- 3 ½ oz.(100g) light muscovado sugar, crumbled
- 3 large eggs,
- 2 tablespoons brandy or cognac (extra to flame)
- 7 ¾ oz.(250g) butter, chilled

Brandy and ginger butter

- 6oz.(175g) unsalted butter, softened
- Grated zest of ½ orange
- 5 tablespoons icing sugar
- 4 tablespoons brandy or cognac
- 2 pieces stem ginger, finely chopped

Method:

- In a bowl add all the ingredients, but the butter and the ingredients for the Brandy/ginger butter.
- Grate ¼ of the butter by holding it by the wrapper.
- Stir for 3-4 minutes.
- Do it again, until all the butter is grated.
- In two greased 34fl.oz. (2 pint) (1.2 l) bowl each, add a round piece of baking paper at the bottom.
- Pour the pudding mixture.
- Add a double layer of baking paper, pleated.

- Tie with a string.
- Place each bowl on foil paper and wrap bringing the edges over the top.
- Place another piece of foil from top to bottom and wrap to make it watertight.
- Place another piece of string to tie up and make a handle.
- Oven steam or boil the pudding for 8 hours.
- Top up the water as required.
- Remove and allow to cool overnight.
- Discard the wrapping and place a new baking paper, foil and string.
- Put away in a dry and cool place until Christmas.
- To serve, prepare the ginger butter by combining all the ingredients.
- Pour over slices of the pudding.

Nutritional Facts

Serves: 8
Calories: 550 Cal
Fat: 25g
Carbohydrate: 77g
Fiber: 2g
Sugar: 16g
Protein: 5g

Vegan Fruit Mince Pies

Ingredients:

- ½ cup white rice flour
- ¼ cup tapioca flour
- ¼ cup chick pea flour
- 1 teaspoon xanthan
- Pinch of salt
- 2oz. (60g) vegan margarine (Nuttelex or similar)
- 4 tablespoons coconut palm sugar
- 1 teaspoon pure vanilla sugar
- 2 tablespoons cold water (filtered)
- 1 teaspoon lemon zest, finely chopped

For filling

- ½ cup grated apple (peeled)
- 2 tablespoons orange zest
- 1 teaspoon lemon zest
- ¼ cup orange juice, freshly squeezed
- 1 cup sultanas
- ½ cup dried apricots
- ½ cup dried cherries
- ½ cup dried cranberries
- ½ cup dried blueberries
- ¼ teaspoon nutmeg
- ¼ teaspoon allspice
- 1 teaspoon cinnamon
- 2 tablespoons maple syrup

Method:

- Pre-heat oven to 350 deg. F (180 deg. C)
- In a bowl sift flours, salt and xanthan.

- In a food processor, add butter, vanilla and sugar and pulse until soft.
- Pour the flour mixture, lemon zest and mix.
- Add water, 1 tablespoon at the time.
- Mold the dough to make it workable and make a ball.
- Wrap the dough with cling wrap and refrigerate for 30 minutes.
- In the meantime, make the filling.
- In a food processor, add all the ingredients and pulse until smooth.
- On a work surface, place pieces of baking paper and roll the dough.
- With a cooking cutter, cut some circles to fit mini muffin tins.
- In 20 greased mini muffin tins, place the circles.
- With a mini star shape cooking cutter, cut some mini stars.
- On a lined baking tray, with baking paper, place the mini stars.
- Place the tray and tins in the oven and cook until browned. (5-10 minutes)
- Place the filling on top of each base and top with a star.

Nutritional Facts

Serves: 20
Calories: 324 Cal
Fat: 9.3g
Carbohydrate: 57.5g
Fiber: 4.0 g
Sugar: 22.5g
Protein: 4.9g

Christmas Pudding Ice-cream

Ingredients:

- 1 orange, juiced
- 1 orange zest
- 5 ¼ oz.(150g) mixed dried fruit
- 2 tablespoons dark rum
- 1/3 cup brandy
- 2 cups thin cream
- 1 cinnamon stick
- 6 eggs yolk
- 1 cup milk
- 1 vanilla bean, split
- ½ cup caster sugar
- 10fl.oz.(300ml) thickened cream, lightly whipped
- ½ teaspoon mixed spice
- Silver dragees and crystallized rose petals to serve

Method:

- In a bowl, add dried fruit, orange zest, rum, orange juice, brandy and refrigerate overnight.
- In a pan, over medium heat, add vanilla bean, milk, cinnamon, thin cream and cook.
- Remove from the heat and put aside.
- In the meantime, in a bowl, add sugar and egg yolks and whisk.
- Pour the warm cream mixture and mix well.
- In another pan, place the mixture and warm again until thickened.
- Place in a low container and allow cooling.
- Fold in the thickened cream, once is cool.
- Place in the freezer until the edges are frozen.
- With an electric mixer, beat and re-freeze again.

- Repeat the process two more times.
- Fold in the macerated fruit.
- Add spices and with the electric mixer, beat again.
- Place in molds and freeze.
- To serve, remove from the mold by inverting onto serving plates. (Dip the bottom of each base in warm water prior inverting to make it easier).
- Sprinkle some dragees and rose petals.

Nutritional Facts

Serves: 7
Calories: 614Cal
Fat: 46g
Carbohydrate: 35 g
Fiber: 0.0g
Sugar: 35g
Protein: 6 g

Raw Food Chocolate Fudge with Chili

Ingredients:

- ½ cup and 2 tablespoons raw cacao powder
- ½ cup raw agave nectar
- ½ cup raw cacao butter
- ½ teaspoon nama shogun
- 2 teaspoons vanilla extract
- Pinch sea salt
- Hot chili pepper or cayenne powder to taste

Method:

- Using a dehydrator or oven to 100 deg. F (40 deg. C), warm cacao butter
- In a food processor, add the cacao butter and pulse for 20 seconds.
- In a pie mold or small molds, pour the mixture.
- Place in the refrigerator for a couple of hours.
- Remove, cut and serve.

Nutritional Facts

Serves: 7
Calories: 86Cal
Fat: 1.1g
Carbohydrate: 21.3 g
Fiber: 1.7 g
Sugar: 18.4 g
Protein: 1.1 g

Raw Food Chocolate Truffles

Ingredients:

- 1 cup dates
- ¼ cup coconut oil
- ½ teaspoon cardamom powder
- ¼ cup agave nectar
- ¼ teaspoon cinnamon
- 1 teaspoon vanilla
- ½ cup raw cacao powder
- ¾ cup soaked nuts (almonds, pecans, walnuts, macadamia), chopped
- ¼ cup dried fruit (blueberries, cranberries, raisins, cherries)
- Pinch sea salt

Method:

- In a food processor, add the dates and pulse for 10 seconds, at high speed.
- Add agave nectar, cinnamon, coconut oil, vanilla, sea salt and cardamom and pulse again for further 10-20 seconds.
- Add the cacao and pulse for another 10 seconds.
- In a bowl, pour the mixture.
- Add the nuts and dried fruit and mix.
- In a lined tray, with an ice cream scooper or spoon, place small size shaped balls of the mixture.
- Place in the refrigerator for a minimum 30 minutes
- Serve.

Nutritional Facts

Serves: 6

Calories: 235Cal
Fat: 12.3g
Carbohydrate: 29.2g
Fiber: 4.9g
Sugar: 21.7g
Protein: 2.4g

Raw Vegan Pumpkin Pie

Ingredients:

Crust

- 2 cups macadamia nuts, walnuts, almonds or any other nuts
- 1 ½ cups medjool dates or similar

Filling

- 4 cups pumpkin cubes, deseeded and peeled
- 1 ½ cups banana slices
- ¾ cup agave nectar
- 1 teaspoon cinnamon
- ¼ teaspoon nutmeg
- ½ teaspoon ground coriander (optional)
- ¼ teaspoon allspice (optional)
- Pinch cayenne (optional)
- 1 tablespoon lemon juice.

Method:

- In a food processor, add the nuts and grind for few seconds.
- Add the dates and pulse again for another 40 seconds.
- Add the agave nectar 1 teaspoon at the time and continue pulsing until the mixture is sticky on the side of the bowl.
- In a pie plate place the crust mixture and press to take the shape of the mold. Set aside.
- In a blender, add all the ingredients to make the filling and blend.
- Pour the mixture over the pie crust and spread evenly.
- Place in the refrigerator for a minimum of 30 minutes
- Serve.

Nutritional Facts

Serves: 10
Calories: 635Cal
Fat: 47.5g
Carbohydrate: 47.8g
Fiber: 8.5g
Sugar: 27.7g
Protein: 24.4g

Steamed Cranberry and Coconut Pudding

Ingredients:

- 5 ½ oz.(160g) soft butter
- 7 ¾ oz.(220g) brown sugar
- 4 ¼ oz.(120g) self-rising flour
- 3 ½ oz.(100g) sultanas
- 7oz.(200g) dried cranberries
- 2oz.(60g) shredded coconut
- 2oz.(60g) fresh breadcrumbs
- 2oz.(50g) almond meal
- 2oz.(50g) almond silvers
- 2 apples, peeled and grated
- 1 orange juice
- 1 orange zest
- ½ teaspoon mixed spice
- 4 eggs
- 2fl.oz.(60ml) dark rum
- 2 limes juice
- 2 lime zest
- 1 teaspoon vanilla extract

Method:

- In a bowl, add 2oz. (60g) butter and 4 ½ oz. (120g) sugar and blend until smooth.
- Sift in flour and mix.
- Add sultanas, coconut, almond meal, almond silvers, cranberries, grated apple, orange juice, orange zest, breadcrumbs, half the rum, eggs, spice, lime juice and zest and mix.
- In a 34 fl. oz. (1 l.) (2pints), greased pudding bowl, place the mixture.
- Wrap with baking paper and tie with a string.

- Steam for 4 hours or check with the skewer.
- In the meantime, prepare the rum butter.
- In a bowl add the remaining butter and sugar and beat.
- Add the rum slowly; pour the remaining rum, vanilla and lemon zest and juice and mix.
- Pour over the pudding to serve.
- Serve.

Nutritional Facts

Serves: 351
Calories: 18.1Cal
Fat: 7.0g
Carbohydrate: 40.4g
Fiber: 3.6 g
Sugar: 24.6g
Protein: 5.8g

Poached Pears

Ingredients:

- 5 Bosc pears, peeled
- ½ bottle port
- ½ bottle red wine
- 9oz.(250g) sugar
- 1 cinnamon stick
- 1 anise star
- Coriander seeds
- 1 Orange zest
- 1 vanilla bean

Method:

- In a pot, add coriander seeds, sugar, star anise, sugar, orange zest, scraped vanilla bean, wine and port.
- Place over medium heat and simmer.
- Add the peeled pears and cover with baking paper, making sure that you cut a small circle in the middle.
- Cover with a lid and cook for 1 hour.

Nutritional Facts

Serves: 5
Calories: 317 Cal
Fat: 0.3g
Carbohydrate: 84.4g
Fiber: 7.5g
Sugar: 70.5g
Protein: 1.0g

Passion Fruit Parfait

Ingredients:

- 1 cup coconut milk
- 3 ½ fl. oz.(100ml) pouring cream
- 4 egg yolks (free range)
- 3 ¼ oz.(90g) caster sugar
- 5fl.oz. (150ml) passion fruit pulp from 8-10 passion fruits

Method:

- In a pot, add cream and coconut milk and bring to the boil. Set aside.
- In a bowl, add sugar and eggs and beat (use electric mixer) until thickened.
- Pour the cream mixture and mix.
- In a pan, over low heat, add the mixture and stir with a wooden spoon. (Ensuring that the mixture does not boil)
- Pour mixture into a bowl and refrigerate overnight.
- Remove from the refrigerator and add passion fruit pulp and mix.
- Place the mixture into a baking dish and freeze.
- From time to time, stir to allow the mixture to be creamy, smooth and frozen.
- Serve in cocktail glasses.

Nutritional Facts

Serves: 5
Calories: 247Cal
Fat: 17.4g
Carbohydrate: 22.0g
Fiber: 1.1g

Sugar: 19.7g
Protein: 3.9g

Grilled Peaches with Mascarpone Cheese

Ingredients:

- 3 peaches, pitted and quartered
- 2 tablespoons sugar
- 2 tablespoons Brandy
- 1 tablespoon fresh lemon juice
- ½ cup mascarpone cheese
- ¼ teaspoon vanilla extract
- ¾ cup dry white wine
- Olive oil to grease

Method:

- In a greased (with olive oil) oven grill rack, at medium heat, place peaches and grill for 2-3 minutes on each side.
- In the meantime, in a bowl, add sugar, lemon juice and Brandy and mix. Set aside.
- Remove the peaches from the grill and place them in a baking dish.
- Pour the brandy mixture and toss.
- Set aside for 15 minutes to marinate. Toss again from time to time.
- In the meantime, in a bowl, add mascarpone and vanilla and combine.
- Serve peaches in dessert dishes, drizzle with wine and place a spoonful of the mascarpone mixture on top.

Nutritional Facts

Serves: 6
Calories: 114Cal
Fat: 2.8g

Carbohydrate: 10.2 g
Fiber: 0.8g
Sugar: 8.5g
Protein: 2.8g

Sweet Potato Crumble

Ingredients:

- 3 pounds ¼ oz. (1 ½ kg) sweet potatoes, peeled and chopped
- 1 tablespoon olive oil
- 6 cloves garlic, crushed
- 2 leeks, cut length ways and thinly sliced
- ½ teaspoon of butter
- ¼ cup cream

Crumble

- 5 ¼ oz. (150g) panko bread crumbs
- 1 tablespoons cold butter
- 1 tablespoon Italian parsley
- 2 tablespoons grated vegetarian parmesan or dairy free parmesan cheese
- ½ cup whole macadamias
- Salt and pepper to taste

Method:

- Pre-heat oven at 350deg. F (180 deg. C).
- In steamer, add sweet potatoes and steam until soft.
- In the meantime, in a large pan, add ¼ teaspoon of butter, garlic and leek and sauté.
- Place the sweet potatoes in the pan, add cream and mash.
- Transfer the mash to a baking tray. Set aside.
- In the meantime prepare the crumble.
- In a food processor, add all the crumble ingredients and pulse.
- Scatter the crumble mixture over the sweet potato mash.
- Place in the oven and cook until golden and crunchy.

Nutritional Facts

Serves: 6
Calories: 547Cal
Fat: 14.5g
Carbohydrate: 94.9g
Fiber: 12.7g
Sugar: 4.7g
Protein: 11.8 g

Thank you

Thank you for reading this book.

I hope you enjoyed it!

If you liked this book I would appreciate if you could take a minute and

leave a review with your feedback.

Look for "Vegetarian Christmas Cookbook"

by Sarah Reed

and

"write a customer review"

Thank you!

Printed in Great Britain
by Amazon